W9-BHY-504

Also by Donald Hall
POETRY

Exiles and Marriages   (1955)
The Dark Houses   (1958)
A Roof of Tiger Lilies   (1964)
The Alligator Bride   (1969)
The Yellow Room   (1971)
A Blue Wing Tilts at the Edge of the Sea   (1975)
The Town of Hill   (1975)
Kicking the Leaves   (1978)

PROSE

String Too Short to Be Saved   (1961)
Writing Well   (1973)
Goatfoot Milktongue Twinbird   (1978)
Remembering Poets   (1978)
The Weather for Poetry   (1982)
Fathers Playing Catch with Sons   (1985)

THE HAPPY MAN

THE HAPPY MAN

POEMS BY

DONALD HALL

RANDOM HOUSE
NEW YORK

Portions of this work were first published, some in
different form, in the following periodicals:
  *The Atlantic, The Iowa Review, The Kenyon Review, The Missouri Review,
The New Criterion, The New Republic, The New Yorker, The Paris Review,
Ploughshares, The Reaper* and *The Virginia Quarterly Review.*
  "Great Day in the Cows' House" first appeared in *The American Poetry
Review* and was later published by Ives St. Press.
  "The Revolution" (originally entitled "A Novel in Two Volumes") first appeared
in *Antaeus.*
  "A Sister by the Pond" (originally entitled "At Eagle Pond") and
"Sums" first appeared in *Poetry.*
  "Twelve Seasons" first appeared in *Twelve Seasons,* published as a limited
edition by Deerfield Press.

Library of Congress Cataloging-in-Publication Data

Hall, Donald, 1928–
  The happy man.

  I. Title.
PS3515.A3152H3 1986   811'.54   86-457
ISBN 0-394-55478-7
ISBN 0-394-74612-0 (pbk.)

Manufactured in the United States of America

Designed by JoAnne Metsch

98765432

First Edition

Behold me then, a man happy and in good health, hiding the rope in order not to hang myself to the rafters of the room where every night I went to sleep alone; behold me no longer shooting, lest I should yield to the too easy temptation . . .

— L E O   T O L S T O Y

CONTENTS

IV
Sisters

I
BARNYARDS

The history was there, in its degree, and one came upon
it in the form of the classic abandoned farm . . .

— HENRY JAMES

GREAT DAY IN THE COWS' HOUSE

In the dark tie-up seven huge Holsteins
lower their heads to feed, chained loosely to old saplings
with whitewashed bark still on them.
They are long dead; they survive, in the great day
that cancels the successiveness of creatures.
Now she stretches her wrinkly neck, her turnip-eye
rolls in her skull, she sucks up breath,
and stretching her long mouth mid-chew she expels:
mm-mmm-mmmmm-mmmmmmmm-ugghwanchhh . . .
—Sweet bellowers enormous and interchangeable,
your dolorous ululations
swell out barnsides, fill spaces inside haymows,
resound down valleys. Moos of revenant cattle
shake ancient timbers and timbers still damp with sap.
*
Now it is warm, late June. The old man strokes
white braids of milk, *strp strp*, from ruminant beasts
with hipbones like tentpoles, the rough
black-and-white hanging crudely upon them.
Now he tilts back his head to recite a poem
about an old bachelor who loves a chicken named Susan.
His voice grows loud with laughter and emphasis
in the silent tie-up where old noises gather.
*
Now a tail lifts to waterfall huge and yellow
or an enormous flop presses out. Done milking, he lifts

with his hoe a leather-hinged board
to scrape manure onto the pile underneath, in April
carted for garden and fieldcorn.

                                  The cows in their house
decree the seasons; spring seeds corn,
summer hays, autumn fences, and winter saws ice
from Eagle Pond, sledging it up hill to pack it away
in sawdust; through August's parch and Indian summer
great chunks of the pond float in the milkshed tank.
*

Pull down the spiderwebs! Whitewash the tie-up!
In the great day there is also the odor of poverty
and anxiety over the Agricultural Inspector's visit.
*

They are long dead; they survive, in the great day
of August, to convene afternoon and morning
for milking. Now they graze Ragged Mountain:—
steep sugarbush, little mountain valleys and brooks,
high clovery meadows, slate-colored lowbush blueberries.
When grass is sweetest they are slow to leave it;
late afternoons he spends hours searching . . .
He knows their secret places; he listens for one peal
of a cowbell carried on a breeze; he calls:
"Ke-bosh, ke-bo-o-sh, ke-bosh, ke-bosh . . ."
He climbs dry creekbeds and old logging roads
or struggles up needle-banks pulling on fir branches.
He hacks with his jackknife a chunk of sprucegum
oozing from bark and softens it in his cheek-pouch
for chewing.

                   Then he pushes through hemlock's gate
to join the society of Holsteins; they look up from grass
as if mildly surprised, and file immediately downward.
*

Late in October after the grass freezes
the cattle remain in their stalls, twice a day loosed
to walk stiff-legged to the watering trough
from which the old man lifts a white lid of ice.
Twice a day he shovels ensilage into their stalls
and shakes hay down from the loft, stuffing a forkful
under each steaming nose.
                    In late winter,
one after one, the pink-white udders
dry out as new calves swell their mothers' bellies.
Now these vessels of hugeness bear, one after one,
skinny-limbed small Holsteins eager to suck
the bounty of freshening. Now he climbs to the barn
in boots and overalls, two sweaters,
a cloth cap, and somebody's old woolen coat;
now he parts the calf from its mother after feeding,
and strips the udder clean,
to rejoice in the sweet frothing tonnage of milk.
*
Now in April, when snow remains on the north side
of boulders and sugar maples, and green
starts from wet earth in open places the sun touches,
he unchains the cows one morning after milking
and lopes past them to open the pasture gate.
Now he returns whooping and slapping their buttocks
to set them to pasture again, and they are free
to wander eating all day long. Now these wallowing
big-eyed calf-makers, bone-rafters for leather,
awkward arks, cud-chewing lethargic mooers
roll their enormous heads, trot, gallop, bounce,
cavort, stretch, leap, and bellow—
as if everything heavy and cold vanished at once
and cow spirits floated
weightless as clouds in the great day's windy April.

When his neighbor discovers him at eighty-seven, his head
leans into the side of his last Holstein;
she has kicked the milkpail over, and blue milk drains
through floorboards onto the manure pile in the great day.

WHIP-POOR-WILL

As the last light
of June withdraws
the whip-poor-will sings
his clear brief notes
by the darkening house, then
rises abruptly from sandy
ground, a brown bird
in the near-night, soaring
over shed and woodshed
to far dark fields. When
he returns at dawn,
in my sleep I hear
his three syllables make
a man's name, who slept
fifty years in this bed
and ploughed these fields:
Wes-ley-Wells ... Wes-
ley-Wells ...
             It is good
to wake early in high
summer with work to do,
and look out the window
at a ghost bird lifting away
to drowse all morning
in his grassy hut.

SCENIC VIEW

Every year the mountains
get paler and more distant—
trees less green, rock piles
disappearing—as emulsion
from a billion Kodaks
sucks color out.
In fifteen years
Monadnock and Kearsarge,
the Green Mountains
and the White will turn
invisible, all
tint removed
atom by atom to albums
in Medford and Greenwich,
while over the valleys
the still intractable granite
rears with unseeable peaks
fatal to airplanes.

NEW ANIMALS

Waking one morning
we cannot find
Kate or Wesley,
or his cows and sheep,
or the hens she looks
after. In my dream
we spend all morning
looking for their old
bodies in tall grass
beside barn
and henyard. Finally
we discover them,
marching up the dirt
road from Andover—
excited, laughing, waving
to catch our attention
as they shepherd
new animals
home to the farm.
They traded Holsteins
and Rhode Island Reds
for zebras, giraffes,
apes, and tigers. They lead
their parade back
to the barn, and the sheep-
dog ostrich

nips at the errant
elephant's heels
and goads the gaudy
heroic lions
and peacocks that keen
AIEE AIEE.

THE ROCKER

"He played jacks with me
after Sunday School,
such a big, gentle boy.
I was ten years
old." The worn-flat
rockers of her chair
bump on the kitchen
floor. "That night they
couldn't find him.
With lanterns the men
climbed the hill
by his mother's house
to look for him; called
his name and stood
listening. Then
their lanterns turned
the windows yellow, one
by one. They told how,
when they climbed up
the attic stairs,
Alexander Blackmore's
nose bumped
into boots swinging."
She's down to eighty
pounds, same as her age,
and her shiny white

fists grip
the rocker's arms.
"He pushed them off
and the boots swung
back and hit him."
Her kettle steams;
her fat old tomcat
turns his head
when a mouse skitters
over linoleum.

THE HENYARD ROUND

1.

From the dark yard by the sheep barn the cock crowed
to the sun's pale
spectral foreblossoming eastward in June,
crowed,

      and crowed,
later each day through fall and winter, conquistador
of January drifts, almost-useless vain strutter
with wild monomaniac eye, burnished swollen chest,
yellow feet serpent-scaled, and bloodred comb,
who mounted with a mighty flutter
his busy hens: Generalissimo Rooster
of nobody's army.

              When he was old we cut his head off
on the sheepyard choppingblock, watching his drummajor
prance, his last resplendent march . . .
As I saw him diminish, as we plucked each feathery badge,
cut off his legs, gutted him,
and boiled him three hours for our fricassee Sunday
dinner, I understood
How the Mighty Are Fallen, and my great-uncle Luther,
who remembered the Civil War,
risen from rest after his morning's sermon, asked
God's blessing on our food.

2.

At the depot in April, parcel post went cheep-cheep
in rectangular cardboard boxes, each
trembling with fifty chicks. When we opened
the carton in the cool toolshed
fifty downed fluffers cheep-cheeping
rolled and teetered.

     All summer it was my chore
to feed them, to water them.
Twice a day I emptied a fouled pan
and freshened it from the trough; twice a day
I trudged up hill to the grainshed, filled
sapbuckets at wooden tubs and poured
grain into v-shaped feeders, watching the greedy
fluster and shove.

     One summer
I nursed a blind chick six weeks—pale yellow,
frail, tentative, meek,
who never ate except when I gapped space for her.
I watched her grow little by little,
but every day outpaced
by the healthy beaks that seized feed
to grow monstrous—and one morning
discovered her dead: meatless, incorrigible . . .

3.

At summer's end the small roosters departed
by truck, squawking. Pullets
moved to the henhouse and extruded each day
new eggs, harvested morning and night. Hens roosted
in darkness locked from skunk and fox,
and let out at dawn footed the brittle yard,
tilting on stiff legs to peck the corncobs
clean; to gobble turnip peels, carrot tops, even
the shells of yesterday's eggs. Hens labored
to fill eggboxes the eggman shipped
to Boston, and to provide our breakfast, gathered
at the square table.
                    When the eggmaking frenzy
ceased, when each in her own time set
for weeks as if setting itself made eggs,
each used-up, diligent hen
danced on the packed soil of the henyard her final
headless jig, and boiled
in her pale shape
                    featherless as an egg, consumed
like the blind chick, like Nannie,
who died one summer at eighty-seven, childish,
deaf, unable to feed herself, demented . . .

TWELVE SEASONS

Snow starts at twilight. All night the house
trembles as ploughs thrust up and down
the highway. Snow keeps on falling—willy-nilly,
irresponsible, letting the wind do its work, gathering
rounded in drifts. Morning flakes
and densens. Overspread by gray and lucid snow,
we sit beside iron stoves
and kettles that steam dry air. At midnight clouds
withdraw, and the full moon relumes
the soft sculpted bowl of this valley.
In the unspotted stillness, in luminous gray shade,
the child's cry opens like a knife-blade.

Old weathered elm chunks, birch still sappy,
oak, maple, ash: irregular slabs of August sun,
ripped from the hill, stacked in the woodshed
with difficulty;—this rummage of slivers, this sprain
of fists, this toe-fracture . . . At bedtime we pile
three split oak logs high in the iron stove.
At six when we open drafts and door in the unbreathing
room, struts of wood unpack in the stove's hollow,
July's green steeple and the acorn tree
dismantle before us, and the sun made solid
transforms into golden heat—like a gift
from August carried by starlight over winter dunes.

Hook a six-pound slab of pale brisket from the barrel's
brine. Bring it to a boil in a great kettle
and pour off the flaky water. Boil it again
four hours and a half. Spiral the peel
from a dense yellow turnip and cleaver it
into eight wedges; drop in the pot for the last
hour's boiling. Ten minutes later put the potatoes in,
scrubbed in their jackets. With half an hour left,
add carrots and the Turkish domes of onions.
For the last twelve minutes lay chunks of cabbage,
green-white and quavering, on the erupting surface
of the inexhaustible pot over the assembling fire.

A doe walks in the railroad's trench on corrupt snow.
Her small hooves poke holes in the crust,
melted and frozen again, that scrapes her ankles
as her starved head swivels for bark. So the dogpack,
loosened one by one from stove-warm houses, gathers
seven leaping bodies that larrup, sliding
along the crust, like twelve-year-old boys at recess
chasing a sissy. They rip her throat out.
Walking on a mild day, as snow melts from the tracks,
we find the body hollowed by birds and coyotes
and drag it aside, into a grove of yellow birch
that beaver forested, leaving spiky stumps behind.

One braid of smoke lifts and undoes itself
over the clapboard cottage of Martha Bates Dudley
all year, keeping nine decades warm in housedress,
slippers, sweater, cardigan, and shawl
as she sits in the tall rocker knitting,
tatting, and crocheting for the fancywork table
at the Church Fair, the first Saturday in August.
Charity occupies a house emptied of talkative dead;
charity occupies a body turned witness of small pains.
When she adds a stick of maple every hour
to her white Glenwood, soup rolls its knuckles
of bubble and froth and works all day without stopping.

Sharpen the scythe with a blue whetstone, wrist
snapping from edge to edge as quick as a hummingbird.
Mow keeping heel to ground or the blade's point
will catch earth; keep feet apart, rocking,
leaning forward; use the steel's weight like a spring
to pull the body forward; sweep back and forth
in a long arc of swaths, in broad semicircles;
march into the wavering field of millet
leaving a swooped line behind you, the mower's
flattened crescents that your ancestors made before you
when they entered Canaan
to husband their land with thighs, shoulders, and forearms.

After supper Belle goes fishing with her Uncle Sherman
in his leaky rowboat, in summer twilight
outlined by gnats. They catch the long silver-pencil
pickerel when they are lucky; suckers, horned pout.
Sherman and Belle dream in their trim-painted boat
of fish dozing in black sleepy water,
and sit in the half-light on motionless water,
alone except for Benjamin Eckersley,
cross-pond in his rowboat, under the faint haze of his pipe.
Whatever they look at speaks to them—the water
in watery speech, birch in the language of birches.
They drift in the boat of their affection.

After two weeks of heat pressing on sweetcorn—
haze dropping on hay, opaque air—this morning wakes
cool with a bright wind, and the mountain
clear, Kearsarge blue under transparent
running air, cold rapid energy sharp as pitchforks.
It is a morning for fires in the stove,
wood's architecture opening shafts and corridors of fire,
vacancies, gases . . . It is a day for clearing
rocks from the fields, volunteers, elm saplings.
Tomorrow we eat the body and drink the blood
in the community of the white church
where the day's pleasure occupies a pew beside suffering.

She works uphill over the ankle-turning stones
of New Canada Road, under yellow birch leaves that start
from ghost trunks. Pausing for breath, she gazes
west into Vermont past bright swampmaples, then climbs
past overgrown appletrees in a double row—
pocked fruit for deer. She finds the gap in the wall
and enters the clearing where a granite doorstep
opens to a cellarhole, shingles collapsed in weed.
Behind the dead elm with its branch for swinging from,
beside the big rock where they played church,
in the stove-in playhouse their father built for them
seventy years ago, her cold sister makes tea.

Now wind rises, and great yellow man-shaped leaves
turn chill air solid, turn air raucous
with leaves calling, calling as each gust starts
a thousand divers and dancers through beaded cold
to their common grave on whitening grass.
Ghosts rise, ghosts whirl in the afternoon leaves,
as the dead visit the declining year. We take them in,
and west of the pond, where the eagle kept house,
yellow light swoops down, turning low hills black
under pale blue that fades into violet; south,
half-dark half-light Kearsarge rises
blinking a cautionary red beam every forty seconds.

At eighty-two, Andy Hunt sits by the stove's fire
he built in morning solitude to warm old bones.
Last summer when he dug worms from fibrous earth
by the woodshed's eighteen-sixty-five oak sill,
he found this oblong rusted box under a foot of dirt,
with two-hundred clay marbles in it—pitted, irregular
greens, pinks, and blues. Andy sits by the stove
and picks the marbles over:—these petrified
flowers of an unrecognizable summer, gathered
by some dead boy, he doesn't know who,
hidden he doesn't know why or when,
and never redeemed unless he redeems them now.

December sun marks cold edges of Kearsarge
and stiff upright cornstalks, gray small trunks
casting shadows hard as maple splinters.
Now the woodchuck sleeps curled in his burrow;
skunk and raccoon are sleeping; snakes
doze in their holes, and bears in shallow recesses.
Now we gather in black evening, in Advent,
as our nervous and reasonable fingers continually reach
for the intangible. Now we wait together;
we add wood to the castiron stove, and midnight's
candlelight trembles on the ceiling
as we drowse waiting. Someone is at the door.

II
SHRUBS
BURNED
AWAY

What then are the situations, from the representation of which, though accurate, no poetical enjoyment can be derived? They are those in which the suffering finds no vent in action; in which a continuous state of mental distress is prolonged, unrelieved by incident, hope, or resistance; in which there is everything to be endured, nothing to be done.

— MATTHEW ARNOLD

Mi-t'o Temple after thirty li. A most desolate spot . . . For fear of them hiding tigers, all trees and shrubs have been burnt.

— HSU HSIA-K'O

Once a little boy and his sister—my mother lay
on top of the quilt, narrow and tense, whispering—
found boards piled up, deep in the woods, and nails,
and built a house for themselves, and nobody knew
that they built their house each day in the woods . . .
I listened and fell asleep, like a baby full of milk,
and carried their house into sleep where I built it
board by board all night, each night
from the beginning; from the pile of boards I built it,
painted it, put doorknobs on it . . .

As I sit by myself, middle-aged in my yellow chair,
staring at the vacant book of the ceiling, starting
the night's bottle, aureoled with cigarette smoke
in the unstoried room, I daydream to build
the house of dying: The old man alone in the farmhouse
makes coffee, whittles, walks, and cuts an onion
to eat between slices of bread. But the white loaf
on the kitchen table comes undone:—Milk leaks
from its side; flour and yeast draw apart;
sugar and water puddle the table's top.

Bullied, found wanting, my father drove home
from his job at the lumberyard weeping,
and shook his fist over my cradle—He'll do
what he wants to do!—and kept to it twenty
years later, still home from work weeping, hopeless
in outrage, smoking Chesterfields, unable to sleep
for coughing. Forty years of waking to shallow light;
forty years of the day's aging; today
I observe for the first time the white hair
that grows from the wrist's knuckle.

I lay in the dark hearing trees scrape
like Hauptmann's ladder on the gray clapboard.
Downstairs the radio diminished, Bing Crosby,
and I heard voices like logs burning, flames
rising and falling, one high and steady, one
urgent and quick. If I cried, if I called . . . I called
softly, sore in the wrapped dark, but there was nothing,
I was nothing, the light's line at the closed door faint.
I called again; I heard her steps:—
Light swept in like a broom from the opening door

and my head lay warm on her shoulder, and her breath
sang in my ear—A Long Long Trail A-winding,
Backward Turn Backward O Time in Your Flight . . .
In the next room a drawer banged shut. When my father
lay dying at fifty-one, he could not deliver
the graduation speech at Putnam Avenue School
near the house he was born in. Taking my father's
place, my head shook like a plucked wire.
I told the fourteen-year-olds:
Never do anything except what you want to do.

"I could not keep from staring out the window.
Teachers told my mother that I was an intelligent girl,
if I would only apply myself. But I continued
to gaze at hills pushing upward, or to draw with my crayons.
In the third grade Mr. Bristol came on Wednesdays;
he said I was the best young artist in the township.
At home when my mother made Parker House Rolls
she let me mold scraps of dough on the oilcloth
of the kitchen table, and I shaped my first soft
rising edible sculptures.

"The year after my father burned in the wrecked car,
my mother came home early from the job she hated
teaching bookkeeping at the secretarial college.
Sometimes she wept because she had flunked someone
she caught cheating. Each day I comforted her;
I was fifteen years old. I cooked supper for her—
hamburgers and hot dogs, baked beans, corn niblets.
Once I took a recipe from *Confidential Chat*,
using asparagus soup, Ritz crackers, and water chestnuts.
She said I would make some man happy.

"That was the year I stopped drawing. Sometimes at night
when she fell asleep I would look at my old portfolio
and cry, and pick up a pencil, and set it down.
Every night before supper we played Chinese checkers
and I beat her; she trembled lifting the marbles, only forty
years old. She came home exhausted, not wanting to play.
After a while we played no more checkers
and she collapsed early with her Agatha Christie
in the blue leather lounger, with the vodka that ruptured
her liver through her abdomen ten years later."

Closing my eyes I collect the others.
One is an actor, homosexual, in a rent-controlled apartment
near Sullivan Square; he waits for the telephone:—
two weeks in *General Hospital* as a kindly
thoracic surgeon. In Woodbridge outside New Haven
another lives—ironic, uxorious, the five children
grown and gone; he waters his lawn with irony; he works
forty hours of irony a week and lives to retire.
Another died dropping from the parking structure in April,
climbing the parapet drunk with purpose.

"When I was twelve I spent the summer on the farm,
painting watercolors all morning, all afternoon hoeing
the garden with my grandmother, who told stories.
We fed the hens; we gathered eggs. Once we discovered
four hen-husks drained dry by a weasel.
That summer I painted One Hundred Views
of house, hill, and covered bridge. When my grandmother
woke me at six o'clock with black coffee
the day lay before me like a green alley over the grass
of a meadow I invented by setting my foot to it.

"When my mother came home from the drying-out hospital,
still convulsive, she took pills and talked without stopping.
She told me about her first breakdown,
when she was nine years old. She had a nightmare
over and over again: Bearded men who looked like the tramps
who asked for bread and butter at the porch door,
or the gypsies who camped in their wagons every summer,
made a circle around her, and the circle grew smaller
as the bearded men shuffled close. Every night
she woke up screaming, unable to stop. She knew:

"They wanted to cut her up for a patchwork quilt. Her mother
and father set a small cot beside their bed, and when she woke
screaming they comforted her. The circle of men
came closer; even when she was awake in her mother's arms,
the circle tightened; she heard her grandfather
tell somebody on the porch, 'We're going to lose
our little girl.' When she stopped crying her mother
pumped a cup of water. She remembered once
her mother brought water in an unwashed coffee cup
and there was sugar stuck in the bottom of the cup."

The Bee Gee, huge engine and tiny stub wings,
snapped around pylons in the Nationals; each year
they clipped more wing off. "On the Fourth of July,
I turned nine years old. I was playing in the woods
with Bingo and Harold Johnson; Bingo had a crush on me.
We were chasing each other and ran into a clearing
and found Bingo and Harold's father and my mother
drunk, rolling in the grass with their clothes off."
Douglas Corrigan took off from Long Island, flight plan
filed for California, plane heavy with gasoline,

and flew to Ireland—Wrong-Way Corrigan:
A mistake, he claimed; no sense of direction . . .
"Later we returned to the house with the grown-ups
and my father threw his Old-Fashioned in my mother's face.
When I tried to run outside my uncle caught me
and set me on his lap; I kept on watching in my blue
shirt over my lace birthday blouse." For three years
David Palmer worked weekends in his garage to build
an airplane using the motors from six lawnmowers.
The CAB refused a license; a strut washed up on Catalina.

"My father ran from the house with a glass in his hand.
When he backed out of the driveway,
he knocked the mailbox over. My mother got my uncle
to chase him along dirt roads at midnight,
very fast;—I sat in the back seat, frightened.
He lost us but we knew where he was going." Wiley Post
and Will Rogers flew from the Walaka Lagoon; Inuits
found their bodies. In the Pacific, Navy patrol-planes
searched for Amelia Earhart while her Lockheed sank
through fathoms with its cargo of helmeted corpses.

The old man walks on blacktop, farm to postoffice,
beside a ditch gray with late August grass. He is
a boy carrying a scythe over blacktop to join
his grandfather on the mowing machine in the hayfield,
where he will trim around rocks. He tilts his blade
toward German prisoners sleeping by day in ditches
who escaped last week from the Canadian prison camp.
When he returns an old man to the farmhouse
by the strong cowbarn, past Aunt Bertha's cottage,
blond prisoners drink schnapps in the livingroom.

I told my wife: Consider me a wind
that lifts square houses up and spins them
into each other; or as a flood loosening houses
from their cellarholes; or as a fire that burns white
wooden houses down. I was content in the dark
livingroom, fixed in the chair with whiskey.
I claimed that the wind was out of control
while I looked through a window where the June tree
blew in the streetlight at two o'clock; leaves broke
from their stems, and the trunk did not split open.

I declared that everywhere at two in the morning
men drank in yellow chairs
while wives lay awake on beds upstairs, necks rigid.
Last night at the reception I glimpsed the made-up faces
of women I knew elsewhere—pale, shaking,
passionate, weeping. We understood together:
The world is a bed. In discontented peace,
in boredom and tolerance, only adultery proves
devotion by risks; only the pulse of betrayal
makes blood pelt in the chest as if with joy.

At the exact millisecond when two cells fused
and multiplied, I started this house. Through years
of milk and potty I constructed foundations. In Miss Ford's
classroom I built it; in vacant lots hopeless at football,
by Blake's Pond hunting for frogs and turtles,
under the leaf's breath, in rotted leaves I built it;
in months at the worktable assembling model airplanes,
at the blackboard doing sums, in blue summer
painting watercolors at my grandmother's I built this house.
I build it now, staring at the wrist-knuckle.

Who is it that sets these words on blue-lined pads?
It is the old man in the room of bumpy wallpaper.
It is the girl who sits on her drunken mother's lap
or carries her grandmother's eggs. It is the boy who reads
The Complete Tales of Edgar Allan Poe. It is
the middle-aged man motionless in a yellow chair,
unable to read, daydreaming the house of dying:—
We take comfort in building this house which does not exist,
because it does not exist, while we stare at the wrist's
hair, drinking Scotch in a yellow chair.

There was the dream of the party: a French farce,
frolic behind curtains, exits and entrances—
like a child fooling parents. I departed
alone on a bus that bumped down the white staircase
of the mansion over the bodies of three women
who stood complacent and pretty in the bus's way,
their faces familiar as photographs. When I looked
back from the bus's rear window at their bodies,
they waved to me although they were dead:—
They forgave me because no one was driving the bus.

My daughter curled in my lap, wailing and red,
eight years old. My thirteen-year-old son's long legs
writhed from a chair as tears fell on his spectacles.
Their father was leaving them . . . I
was leaving them. Their muscles contracted
knees to chin, as I watched from my distance,
and their limbs twitched and jerked in the velvet room.
My daughter wanted to see the place I had rented
to move to. She whirled among cheap furniture,
over bare linoleum, saying, "Cozy, *cozy* . . ."

It rains on Sunset Boulevard. I walk with the collar
of my jacket turned up. Topless go-go dancers twist
at the back of a bar, while men on the wet sidewalk
peer into the doorway at the young women's bodies,
their smooth skin intolerably altered by ointments
and by revolving orange and purple lights.
Lights bruise their thighs:—for three thousand years
these lights and ointments . . . I discarded
the comforts I contrived for myself; or I exchanged them
for a rain of small faces on the abandoned street.

I am a dog among dogs, and I whine
about waking to the six o'clock sun of summer,
or brag about Sinbad's adventures, for which I left
houses excessive with shrubbery, carpets, and mirrors.
Justifying myself I claim: From the breathless blue
of my father's face I chose
the incendiary flower, yellow fire and therefore
rain on the Boulevard. Now in the gray continuous
morning, water drips from the cindery house that wanted
to bloom in the night. I stay up all night

at the Hollywood–La Brea Motel looking at television,
black-and-white war movies, Marines at Iwo,
sailors and blondes, B-24s; I do not understand
what happens. I listen to shills in blazers
with sixpenny London accents pitch acrylic while I drink
Scotch from the bottle. Studying a bikini'd
photograph on a matchbox, I dial BONNIE FASHION
MODEL AVAILABLE at four in the morning
from my vinyl room, and the answering service tells me
that Bonnie is out to lunch . . .

"I wait for the plane inside a blockhouse
at the airport's edge; then the cement walls vibrate
as if an earthquake shook them. I understand at once:
The plane from Ireland has crashed trying to land.
Immediately I watch a conveyor belt
remove bodies covered with brown army blankets
from the broken snake of the fuselage. One of the dead
sits up abruptly, points a finger at me,
and stares accusingly. It is an old man with an erection;
then I notice that all of the dead are men."

Another self sits all day in a watchpocket
of cigarette smoke, staring at the wrist-knuckle,
in repetitious vacancy examining the ceiling, its cracks
and yellowed paint, unprinted emptiness rolling
as continuous as the ocean, no ship or landfall anywhere,
no bird or airplane. I climb from the yellow chair
to the bare bedroom and lie on my back smoking
and staring . . . until ice in a glass, golden whiskey,
euphoria, falling down, and sleep with two yellowjacketed
Nembutals pave the undreaming gilt road to nothing.

Therefore I envy the old man hedging and ditching
three hundred years ago in Devon. I envy the hedge
and the ditch. When my father came home
from the lumberyard, head shaking, fingers
yellow with Chesterfields, I begged him to play catch
with me. He smacked the pocket
of a catcher's mitt: "Put her there!"—and I threw
a fastball ten feet over his head. As he trotted
after the ball I waited, ashamed of being
wild: enraged, apologetic, unforgiving.

Now I prepare to walk the dirt road by the pond.
I prepare to enter the sand. I endure
the present of Laurel Canyon among the middle-aged
rich who eat shrimp curled on ice, who wear tartan
jackets and earrings coded to shoes. They do not notice
when I go back down to the cellar under the kitchen
where a mirror hangs in the gloom. I make out
a white beard and glasses that reflect nothing:
But when I touch my chin my face is smooth.
I rejoin the party; I smile; I am careful drinking . . .

Nothing remains except a doll strangled on fencewire.
Night after night I sleep on pills
and wake exhausted. Rage scrapes its iron across my chest.
I cannot enter the farmhouse in the hills, or find the road
vanished under burdock. I burn another house
and self-pity exhausts me. I pour the first tumbler
over ice cubes that dull the taste. Roots of my hair
go numb. Numbness spreads downward
over the forehead's wrinkles past bloody eyes
to stomach, to wrist's white hair, to dead penis.

The world is a bed, I announce; my love agrees.
A hundred or a thousand times our eyes encounter;
each time the clothes slough off, anatomies
of slippery flesh connect again
on the world's bed, and the crescent of nerves
describes itself again in the wretched
generality of bliss. If we are each the same
on the world's bed, if we are each manikins of the other,
then the multitude is one and one is the multitude;
many and one we perform procedures of comfort.

I am very happy. I dance supine on my bed laughing
until four in the morning, when the bottle is empty
and the liquor store closed on Hollywood and La Brea.
I must not drive the car for cigarettes;—
therefore I lurch a mile to the All-Nite Laundro-Mart
and falter back coughing. In the morning I lie
waking dozing twisted in the damp clothes
of lethargy, loathing, and the desire to die.
My father's head shakes like a plucked wire.
Never do anything except what you want to do.

"I am sad in the convenient white kitchen, dreaming
that I weep as I start making dinner.
The children themselves weep, bringing their sentences
on small folded squares of blue paper.
They will take pills to die without disturbance.
I help them count the pills out, and arrange
pillows for their comfort as they become sleepy.
While I slice onions and peppers on the breadboard,
someone whose identity hovers just out of sight, the way
a beekeeper's mask darkens a face,

"walks up the busy street and enters the kitchen
to instruct me in butchering the children.
The visitor picks up the long rag doll and with scissors
carefully cuts the doll's limbs at the joints,
teaching me expertly, with anatomical explanations
and a scientific vocabulary, while cutting and preparing
the model, then places the doll's parts
on a high shelf, arranged with the gaps of dismemberment
visible, so that I may consult it while cutting,
as I must do, as it seems that I want to do."

III

MEN

DRIVING

CARS

The Electress Dowager, one day when Luther was dining with her, said to him: "Doctor, I wish you may live forty years to come." "Madam," replied he, "rather than live forty years more, I would give up my chance of Paradise."

—WILLIAM JAMES

MR. WAKEVILLE ON INTERSTATE 90

"Now I will abandon the route of my life
as my shadowy wives abandon me, taking my children.
I will stop somewhere. I will park in a summer street
where the days tick like metal in the stillness.
I will rent the room over Bert's Modern Barbershop
where the TO LET sign leans in the plateglass window;
or I will buy the brown BUNGALOW FOR SALE.

"I will work forty hours a week clerking at the paintstore.
On Fridays I will cash my paycheck at Six Rivers Bank
and stop at Harvey's Market and talk with Harvey.
Walking on Maple Street I will speak to everyone.
At basketball games I will cheer for my neighbors' sons.
I will watch my neighbors' daughters grow up, marry,
raise children. The joints of my fingers will stiffen.

"There will be no room inside me for other places.
I will attend funerals regularly and weddings.
I will chat with the mailman when he comes on Saturdays.
I will shake my head when I hear of the florist
who drops dead in the greenhouse over a flat of pansies;
I spoke with her only yesterday . . .
When lawyer elopes with babysitter I will shake my head.

"When Harvey's boy enlists in the Navy
I will wave goodbye at the Trailways Depot with the others.
I will vote Democratic; I will vote Republican.
I will applaud the valedictorian at graduation
and wish her well as she goes away to the university
and weep as she goes away. I will live in a steady joy;
I will exult in the ecstasy of my concealment."

SUMS

[from *"The Daye-Boke of Adam Raison"* (1515–1560)]

From that daye thee Hart strokys
his meeter. Kingesguard sette us
at Rodesyde while they stepd himm
past us in his whyte Veste:
Necke stode free of its Collare
for thee Axe at thee 8e Belle.

Somme theyre cryed: "Kingeslayer
Piggeshart!" Boyes through Turdes
striking his Bodye striding—
his Feete wide to balance himm,
his Handes thongedd thigither—
the laste Rodd of his Manhode.

In his Necke a blew Veyne throbbd
thee Hartsblodde—*onne*, and *onne*—
as if to rekkon Summes. Then Knees
bangd on Wode of Scaffholde,
Axemann gruntyd, glintt of bryght
Blade. Blodde-russhe.

THE REVOLUTION

In the Great Hall where Lady Ann by firelight after dining alone
nodded and dreamed that her cousin Rathwell turned into a unicorn,
and woke shuddering, and was helped to her chambers, undressed,
and looked after, and in the morning arose to read Mrs. Hemans,
sitting prettily on a garden bench, with no sound disturbing
her whorled ear but the wind and the wind's apples falling,
                                       the servants

tended fires, answered bells, plucked grouse, rolled sward, fetched
eggs, clipped hedge, mended linen, baked scones, and served tea.
While Lady Ann grew pale playing the piano, and lay late in bed aging,
she regretted Rathwell who ran off to Ceylon with his indescribable
desires, and vanished—leaving her to the servants who poached, larked,
drank up the cellar, emigrated without notice, copulated, conceived,
                              and begot us.

COUPLET

Old Timers' Day, Fenway Park, 1 May 1982

When the tall puffy
figure wearing number
nine starts
late for the fly ball,
laboring forward
like a lame truckhorse
startled by a gartersnake,
—this old fellow
whose body we remember
as sleek and nervous
as a filly's—

and barely catches it
in his glove's
tip, we rise
and applaud weeping:
On a green field
we observe the ruin
of even the bravest
body, as Odysseus
wept to glimpse
among shades the shadow
of Achilles.

THE BASEBALL PLAYERS

Against the bright
grass the white-knickered
players tense, seize,
and attend. A moment
ago, outfielders
and infielders adjusted
their clothing, glanced
at the sun and settled
forward, hands on knees;
the pitcher walked back
of the hill, established
his cap and returned;
the catcher twitched
a forefinger; the batter
rotated his bat
in a slow circle. But now
they pause: wary,
exact, suspended—

               while
abiding moonrise
lightens the angel
of the overgrown
garden, and Walter Blake
Adams, who died at
fourteen, waits
under the footbridge.

MY FRIEND FELIX

"Beginning at five o'clock, just before dawn rises
in the rearview mirror, I drive at eighty, alone,
all day through Texas. I am a pencil extending
a ruler's line to the unchangeable horizon
west as I repeat a thousand quarrels with my wives.
My grip on the steering wheel slackens; my mind's voice turns
mild and persuasive, quietly addressing the young
doctor at the detox center . . . But I cannot stop
hearing again, word-for-word, last winter's two o'clock
call from a motel in Albany—she would not say
where she was—as my daughter wept, sighed, begged forgiveness,
and allowed the telephone to drop from her fingers.
When I have driven straight through daylight, five-foot neon
letters rise crimson in the pale west: BAR. Thirty years
drown: I am a young man again driving with Felix
from New Haven to San Diego where he will join
his Crusader and his carrier, and in two months
overshoot the runway and slide to the Pacific's
silt bottom without jettisoning his canopy,
while a helicopter hovers an hour above him.
For a moment Felix sits alongside me again,
a young man forever, with his skin wrinkled and puffed
from thirty years of soaking in his watery chair:
All day we drove west on a ruled highway: At a BAR
we swallowed two pitchers, and back on the road again
I pulled out to pass a tractor-trailer. Another

approached and neither truck would give way; I labored past
the semi inch-by-inch and at the last half-second
sideslipped in front. As our pulses slowed we stared ahead,
and from the slipcovered seat beside me Felix spoke:
'The time that we lose, by stopping to drink, we make up
by drunken driving.' Continuing straight west I dream
of my lucky friend Felix the singlewing halfback."

MERLE BASCOM'S .22

"I was twelve when my father gave me this .22
Mossberg carbine—hand-made, with a short octagonal
barrel, stylish as an Indianfighter posing
for a photograph. We ripped up Bokar coffeecans
set into the sandbank by the track—competitive
and companionable. He was a good shot, although
his hands already trembled. Or I walked with my friend
Paul who loved airplanes and wanted to be a pilot,
and carried my rifle loosely, pointing it downward;
I aimed at squirrels and missed. Later I shot woodchucks
that ate my widowed mother's peas and Kentucky
Wonders when I visited on weekends from college,
or drove up from my Boston suburb, finding the gun
in its closet behind the woodstove. Ten years ago
my mother died; I sold up, and moved here with my work
and my second wife, gladly taking my tenancy
in the farmhouse where I intended to live and die.
I used my rifle on another generation
of woodchucks that ate our beans. One autumn an old friend
from college stayed with us after a nervous breakdown:
trembling from electroshock, depressed, suicidal.
I wrapped the octagonal Mossberg in a burlap
bag and concealed it under boards in the old grainshed.
In our quiet house he strengthened and stopped shaking.
When he went home I neglected to retrieve my gun,
and the next summer woodchucks took over the garden.

I let them. Our lives fitted mountain, creek, and hayfield.
Long days like minnows in the pond quickened and were still.
When I looked up from Plutarch another year had passed.
One Sunday the choir at our church sang Whittier's hymn
ending with 'the still small voice of calm.' Idly I thought,
'I must ask them to sing that hymn at my funeral.'
Soon after, I looked for the .22 in the shed,
half expecting it to have vanished, but finding it
wrapped intact where I left it, hardly rusted. I spent
a long evening taking it apart and cleaning it;
I thought of my father's hands shaking as he aimed it.
Then I restored the Mossberg to its accustomed place
in the closet behind the stove. At about this time
I learned that my daughter-in-law was two months pregnant:
It would be the first grandchild. One day I was walking
alone and imagined a granddaughter visiting:
She loved the old place; she swam in the summer pond with us;
she walked with us in red October; she grew older, she fell
in love with a neighbor, she married . . . As I daydreamed,
suddenly I was seized by a fit of revulsion:
I thought: 'Must I go through all that again? Must I live
another twenty years?' It was as if a body
rose from a hole where I had buried it years ago
while my first marriage was twisting and thrashing to death.
One night I was drunk and lost control of my Beetle
off 128 near my ranchhouse. I missed a curve
at seventy miles an hour and careened toward a stone wall.
In a hundredth of a second I knew I would die;
and, as joy fired through my body, I knew something else.
But the car slowed itself on rocks and settled to rest
between an elm and a maple; I sat breathing,
feeling the joy leach out, leaving behind the torment
and terror of my desire. Now I felt this affliction
descend again and metastasize through my body.

Today I drove ninety miles, slowly, seatbelt fastened,
to North Andover and Paul's house, where he lives flying
out of Logan for United. I asked him to hide
the firing pin of an octagonal .22.
He nodded and took it from my hands without speaking.
I cannot throw it away; it was my father's gift."

IV
SISTERS

If I were asked to tell the truth about God's purposes, when he created us, I would say: "Repose." If I were asked what the soul looked for I would answer: "Repose." If I were asked what all creatures wanted, in all their natural efforts and motions, I would answer: "Repose."

— MEISTER ECKHART

A SISTER ON THE TRACKS

Between pond and sheepbarn, by maples and watery birches,
Rebecca paces a double line of rust
in a sandy trench, striding on black
creosoted eight-by-eights.
                              In nineteen-forty-three,
wartrains skidded tanks,
airframes, dynamos, searchlights, and troops
to Montreal. She counted cars
from the stopped hayrack at the endless crossing:
ninety-nine, one-hundred . . . and her grandfather Ben's
voice shaking with rage and oratory told
how the mighty Boston and Maine
kept the Statehouse in its pocket.
                              Today Rebecca walks
a line that vanishes, in solitude
bypassed by wars and commerce. She remembers the story
of the bunting'd day her great-great-great-
grandmother watched the first train roll and smoke
from Potter Place to Gale
with fireworks, cider, and speeches. Then the long rail
drove west, buzzing and humming; the hive of rolling stock
extended a thousand-car'd perspective
from Ohio to Oregon, where men who left stone farms
rode rails toward gold.
                              On this blue day she walks
under a high jet's glint of swooped aluminum pulling

its feathery contrail westward. She sees ahead
how the jet dies into junk, and highway wastes
like railroad. Beside her the old creation retires,
hayrack sunk like a rowboat
under its fields of hay. She closes her eyes
to glimpse the vertical track that rises
from the underworld of graves,
soul's ascension connecting dead to unborn, rails
that hum with a hymn of continual vanishing
where tracks cross.
              For she opens her eyes to read
on a solitary gravestone next to the rails
the familiar names of Ruth and Matthew Bott, born
in a Norfolk parish, who ventured
the immigrant's passionate Exodus westward to labor
on their own land. Here love builds
its mortal house, where today's wind carries
a double scent of heaven and cut hay.

FOR AN EXCHANGE OF RINGS

They rise into mind,
the young lovers
of eighteen-nineteen:
As they walk together
in a walled garden
of Hampstead, tremulous,
their breathing quick,
color high, eyes lucent,
he places the floral
ring with its almondine
stone on her finger.
Although in two winters,
hopeless in Rome,
her letters unopened
beside him, he will
sweat, cough, and die;
although forty years
later a small old
woman will wear
his ring and locket
of hair as she stops
breathing—now, in
Hampstead, in eighteen-
nineteen, they are

wholly indifferent
to other days as they
moisten and swell.

THE IMPOSSIBLE MARRIAGE

The bride disappears. After twenty minutes of searching
we discover her in the cellar, vanishing against a pillar
in her white gown and her skin's original pallor.
When we guide her back to the altar, we find the groom
in his slouch hat, open shirt, and untended beard
withdrawn to the belltower with the healthy young sexton
from whose comradeship we detach him with difficulty.
O never in all the cathedrals and academies
of compulsory Democracy and free-thinking Calvinism
will these poets marry!—O pale, passionate
anchoret of Amherst! O reticent kosmos of Brooklyn!

ACORNS

An oak twig drops
in the path as we climb
the slippery needled
slope from the pond: nine

flame-shaped leaves,
glossy, with yellow-
green sinews veering
out from red spines;

under the leaves, two
acorns depart
from woody cups:
shiny, metallic,

verdant, as acorn-
meat presses from
inside out, volume
thrusting to smooth

the tumid surface
of tiny mast-woman
breasts, nipple-
points centering pale

aureoles. We climb
slowly, carrying
a wicker basket up
the slippery path.

GRANITE AND GRASS

1

On Ragged Mountain birches twist from rifts in granite.
Great ledges show gray through sugarbush. Brown bears
doze all winter under granite outcroppings or in cellarholes
the first settlers walled with fieldstone.
Granite markers recline in high abandoned graveyards.

Although split by frost or dynamite, granite is unaltered;
earthquakes tumble boulders across meadows; glaciers
carry pebbles with them as they grind south
and melt north, scooping lakes for the Penacook's trout.
Stone bulks, reflects sunlight, bears snow, and persists.

When highway-makers cut through a granite hill, scoring
deep trench-sides with vertical drillings, they leave behind
glittering sculptures, monuments to the granite state
of nature, emblems of permanence
that we worship in daily disease, and discover in stone.

2.
But when we climb Ragged Mountain past cordwood stumpage,
over rocks of a dry creekbed, in company of young hemlock,
only granite remains unkind. Uprising in summer, in woods
and high pastures, our sister the fern breathes, trembles,
and alters, delicate fronds outspread and separate.

The fox pausing for scent cuts holes in hoarfrost.
Quail scream in the fisher's jaw; then the fisher dotes.
The coy-dog howls, raising puppies that breed more puppies
to rip the throats of rickety deer in March.
The moose's antlers extend, defending his wife for a season.

Mother-and-father grass lifts in the forsaken meadow,
grows tall under sun and rain, uncut, turns yellow,
sheds seeds, and under assault of snow relents; in May
green generates again. When the bear dies, bees construct
honey from nectar of cinquefoil growing through rib-bones.

3.
Ragged Mountain was granite before Adam divided.
Grass lives because it dies. If weary of discord
we gaze heavenward through the same eye that looks at us,
vision makes light of contradiction:
Granite is grass in the holy meadow of the soul's repose.

A SISTER BY THE POND

1.

An old *Life* photograph
prints itself on Rebecca's mind: The German
regular army hangs
partisans on the Russian front.
Grandfather Wehrmacht in his tight-
collared greatcoat adjusts
the boy's noose as his elderly
adjutant watches. Beside the boy,
his girl companion has already
strangled, her gullet cinched when a soldier
kicked the box from her feet.
In the photograph, taken
near Minsk, gray sky behind him
the summer of nineteen-forty-one,
the boy smiles—
as if he understood that being hanged
is no great matter.

2.

At this open winter's end, in the wrack
and melt of April,
Rebecca walks on the shore by her summer
swimming place, by Eagle Pond
where the ice rots. Over
the pocked glaze, puddles of gray stain
spread at mid-day. Every year
an ice-fisherman waits one weekend
too many, and his shack drowns
among reeds and rowboats. She counts
the season's other
waste: mostly the beaver's work—stout
trees chewed through, stripped
of bark, trailing
twigs in the water. Come summer,
she will drag away the trash, and loll on red
blossoms of moss.

3.

She walks on the shore today
by "Sabine," the beach her young
aunts made, where they loafed together,
hot afternoons of the war. She arranged
freshwater mussels on moss;
watched a mother duck
lead her column; studied the quick
repose of minnows; lying on pine needles loosened
out of her body. Forty years
later Rebecca walks
by the same water: When July's lilies
open in the cove
by the boggy place where bullfrogs
bellow, they gather the sun
as they did when she picked a bunch
for her grandfather Ben
in his vigorous middle age.

4.

In October she came here last,
strolling by pondside with her daughter,
whose red hair brightened
against black-green fir.
Rebecca gazed at her daughter's pale
watery profile, admiring the forehead broad
and clear like Ben's, without guile,
and took pleasure in the affection
of her silent company. By the shore
a maple stood upright,
casting red leaves, its trunk gnawed
to a three-inch waist
of centerwood that bore the branches'
weight. Today when she looks for it, it
is eaten all the way down; blond splinters
show within the gray
surface of the old chewing.

5.

Two weeks ago she drove her daughter
to the Hematology Clinic
of the Peter Bent Brigham Hospital
and paced three hours
among bald young women and skeletal boys
until a resident spoke
the jargon of reassurance. By the felled
maple Rebecca's heart
sinks like the fisherman's shack. She sees again
her son's long body twist
in the crushed Fiesta: A blue light revolves
at three in the morning; white-coated helpers
lift him onto a stretcher;
the pulverized windshield glitters
on black macadam
and in the abrasions of his face.

6.

In the smile of the boy hanged
near Minsk, and in the familiar entropy
of April at Eagle Pond,
she glimpses ahead a winter
of skeleton horses in electric snow.
That April, only the deep burrow-hiders
will emerge who slept
below breath and nightmare: Blacksnake,
frog, and woodchuck
take up their customs among milkweed
that rises through bones
of combines. That summer, when blackberries
twist from the cinders
of white houses, the bear
will pick at the unripe fruit
as he wastes and grows thin, fur
dropping off in patches from his gray skin.

7.

Today, at the pond's edge, old
life warms from the suspense of winter.
Pickerel hover under the pitted, corrupt
surface of April ice
that erodes at the muddy shoreline
where peepers will sing
and snapping turtles bury their eggs.
She sways in the moment's trembling
skin and surge: She desires only
repose, wishing to rise
as the fire wishes or to sink
with the wish and nature of stones.
She wants her soul to loosen
from its body, to lift into sky
as a bird or withdraw as a fish into water
or into water itself
or into weeds that waver in water.

THE DAY I WAS OLDER

The Clock
The clock on the parlor wall, stout as a mariner's clock,
disperses the day. All night it tolls the half-hour
and the hour's number with resolute measure,
approaching the poles and crossing the equator
over fathoms of sleep. Warm
in the dark next to your breathing,
below the thousand favored stars, I feel
horns of gray water heave
underneath us, and the ship's pistons
pound as the voyage continues over the limited sea.

The News
After tending the fire, making coffee, and pouring milk
for cats, I sit in a blue chair each morning,
reading obituaries in the *Boston Globe*
for the mean age; today there is MANUFACTURER CONCORD 53,
EX-CONGRESSMAN SAUGUS 80—and I read
that Emily Farr is dead, after a long illness in Oregon.
Once in an old house we talked for an hour, while a coalfire
brightened in November twilight and wavered
our shadows high on the wall
until our eyes fixed on each other. Thirty years ago.

The Pond

We lie by the pond on a late August afternoon
as a breeze from low hills in the west stiffens water
and agitates birch leaves yellowing above us.
You set down your book
and lift your eyes to white trunks tilting from shore.
A mink scuds through ferns; an acorn tumbles.
Soon we will turn to our daily business.
You do not know that I am watching, taking pleasure
in your breasts that rise and fall as you breathe.
Then I see mourners gathered by an open grave.

The Day

Last night at suppertime I outlived my father, enduring
the year, month, day, and hour
when he lay back on a hospital bed in the guestroom
among cylinders of oxygen—mouth open, nostrils and lips
fixed unquivering, pale blue. Now I have wakened
more mornings to frost whitening the grass,
read the newspaper more times, and stood more times,
my hand on a doorknob without opening the door.
Father of my name, father of long fingers, I remember
your dark hair, and your face almost unwrinkled.

The Cup
From the Studebaker's backseat, on our Sunday drives,
I watched her earrings sway. Then I walked uphill
beside an old man carrying buckets
under birches on an August day. Striding at noontime,
I looked at wheat and at river cities. In the crib
my daughter sighed opening her eyes. I kissed the cheek
of my father dying. By the pond an acorn fell.
You listening here, you reading these words as I write them,
I offer this cup to you: Though we drink
from this cup every day, we will never drink it dry.

The passage quoted from Meister Eckhart is cut down from the original. Other borrowings from Eckhart occur in "Great Day in the Cows' House," "Twelve Seasons," "Granite and Grass," and the two Sister poems.

"Shrubs Burned Away" is the first part of a long poem called *Build a House*. There will be two more sections of roughly the same length.

This book is dedicated to Jane Kenyon, who has been the first to read all the poems. I am as always grateful to Robert Bly, Galway Kinnell, W. D. Snodgrass, and Louis Simpson. For this book I am indebted also to Tom Clark, Liam Rector, Robert Pinsky, Wesley McNair, Joyce Peseroff, Gregory Orr, Caroline Finkelstein, Cynthia Huntington, Lloyd Schwartz, and Marty Lammon. Frank Bidart read this manuscript several times and by his comments altered it. For help with particular poems I am grateful to Michael Cuddihy and Sam Hamill.

DONALD HALL is one of America's most prolific and admired men of letters. *THE HAPPY MAN* is his eighth book of poems. His first, *EXILES AND MARRIAGES*, was published in 1955 and won the Lamont prize for that year. Other collections of poems include *A ROOF OF TIGER LILIES* (1964), *THE ALLIGATOR BRIDE* (1969), *THE TOWN OF HILL* (1975), and *KICKING THE LEAVES* (1978). He is also the author of many works of prose, among them *REMEMBERING POETS* (1978), *STRING TOO SHORT TO BE SAVED* (1962), and *FATHERS PLAYING CATCH WITH SONS* (1985), and has also written drama, criticism, literature for children, and edited several anthologies. Mr. Hall and his wife, the poet Jane Kenyon, live in New Hampshire, the state which he serves as poet laureate, on a farm that has been in his family for well over a century.